What was it like in the past...?

At home

Heinemann
LIBRARY

Mandy Ross

H www.heinemann.co.uk/library
Visit our website to find out more information about Heinemann Library books.

To order:
☎ Phone 44 (0) 1865 888066
▤ Send a fax to 44 (0) 1865 314091
💻 Visit the Heinemann Bookshop at www.heinemann.co.uk/library to browse our catalogue and order online.

First published in Great Britain by Heinemann Library, Halley Court, Jordan Hill, Oxford OX2 8EJ, a division of Reed Educational and Professional Publishing Ltd. Heinemann is a registered trademark of Reed Educational & Professional Publishing Ltd.

OXFORD MELBOURNE AUCKLAND JOHANNESBURG BLANTYRE
GABORONE IBADAN PORTSMOUTH (NH) USA CHICAGO

© Reed Educational and Professional Publishing Ltd 2003
The moral right of the proprietor has been asserted.

Designed by Celia Floyd
Originated by Ambassador Litho Ltd
Printed in Hong Kong/China

ISBN 0 431 14826 0   (hardback)   ISBN 0 431 14836 8   (paperback)
07 06 05 04 03   07 06 05 04 03
10 9 8 7 6 5 4 3 2   10 9 8 7 6 5 4 3 2 1

British Library Cataloguing in Publication Data
Ross, Mandy
    Homes. – (What was it like in the past?)
1. Dwellings – History – Juvenile literature
I. Title
643.1'09

Acknowledgements
Quotation on page 7 from 'Birmingham Voices' by Helen Lloyd and Lucy Harland, Tempus Publishing and BBC Radio WM 'The Century Speaks', 1999; pages 9, 10, 15, 21 from 'Homes for People' by Carl Chinn, Brewin Books, 1999; page 13 from 'Finding out about women in Twentieth Century Britain' by Sarah Harris, BT Batsford Ltd, 1989; page 18 from 'How we used to live 1954-70' by Freda Kelsall, A & C Black, 1987.
The Publishers would like to thank the following for permission to reproduce photographs:
Advertising Archives: 22; BBC Photograph Library: 20; Beamish Museum: 8; Camera Press: 25; Corbis: 4; Courtesy of English Partnerships/Henderson: 29; Edifice: 10; Hulton Archive: 6, 9, 11, 12, 13, 14, 15, 17, 18, 21; Lefauconnier Jerrican: 5; London Aerial Photo Library: 23; Network/Mark Power: 24; Popperfoto: 7; Powerstock Zefa: 26; Rex: 19; Topham: 16, 27, 28.
Cover photograph reproduced with permission of Popperfoto.

Our thanks to Stuart Copeman for his help in the preparation of this book.
Every effort has been made to contact copyright holders of any material reproduced in this book. Any omissions will be rectified in subsequent printings if notice is given to the Publisher.

Contents

Words printed in **bold letters like these** are explained in the Glossary.

Each **decade** is highlighted on a timeline at the bottom of the page.

Then and now

Does your home have electricity and central heating? In 1900, very few homes had electricity, central heating, indoor toilets or bathrooms.

In 1900 the homes of rich and poor people were very different. Rich people lived in large, comfortable houses, with many servants. Most poor people lived in unhealthy, cramped conditions.

In the early 1900s, families used to sit around the table to eat their tea.

Today's family meals can be very different from those in the 1900s.

In the 1900s, almost everyone (except the very wealthy) **rented** their homes from private owners called landlords.

This book looks at how homes have changed over the past hundred years. It also looks at the differences between the homes of rich and poor people.

1900s: Rich and poor

In 1900, millions of people in Britain lived in bad conditions. In cities and towns, poor people lived in crowded badly-built **terraced** houses.

Several families might share an outside toilet and a water **pump** in the yard. The water supply was often dirty. Pests, such as cockroaches or rats, lived in many houses.

Poor families often had to live in just one room.

In the countryside it was just as bad. Farmworkers lived in cottages owned by the landowner. If they lost their job, they lost their home too.

In contrast, rich families lived in comfort in large houses. Some already had electric lights.

Richer families had big, comfortable homes. Beautiful wallpaper and heavy, dark furniture looked very grand.

1910s: Work and leisure

In 1910, running a home was hard work without electrical goods such as washing machines. Women and children did most of the work. Do you help with the housework? Do you use any machines?

Every morning the fire or grate had to be cleared and lit. Food was bought fresh each day, because there were no refrigerators or freezers.

Servants used a washing tub and irons heated on the grate. Poorer women did the work themselves.

> *Remembering washday:*
> 'You had to fetch the water, and light a coal fire to boil it. Then you washed the clothes by hand, put them through the mangle to squeeze the water out, and hung them out to dry.'

The **First World War** began in 1914. It brought many changes. As the men went to fight, women took over their jobs. But they still had to do the work at home, too.

Before television or radio, families made their own entertainment.

1920s: Homes fit for heroes

After the **First World War**, the **government** set out to build 'homes fit for heroes'. Thousands of pleasant new **council** houses were built to end the housing shortage. But often the poorest people had to stay on in unhealthy housing.

Many new houses were built in the 1920s.

A council leader welcomed back soldiers: 'We cannot let our heroes come home from horrible, water-logged trenches to something little better than a pigsty here.'

A family listening to the radio, or wireless, as it was called then. The BBC started radio broadcasts in 1922.

Electrical goods such as heaters and vacuum cleaners went on sale, but only wealthier people could afford them. It was many years until everyone had electricity at home. Which electric machines do you have in your house?

1930s: The suburbs

In the 1930s, new houses with gardens were built outside the city centre. These areas were called suburbs. The streets were broad, and planted with trees. Do you live in a suburb?

People were glad to move out of the inner city. They enjoyed living in these light, roomy houses. Gardening became a popular hobby.

Many new homes in the suburbs had gardens and people could park their cars in the drive.

But many people were still living in poor conditions in towns and cities. In the 1930s, many people lost their jobs, and so they lost their homes, too, because they could not pay the **rent**.

In the 1930s, many people still had to wash in a tin bath in front of the fire.

Bath night – with no bathroom:
'Saturday night was bath night in a tin bath in the kitchen... Mum used to heat the water in the big iron saucepans on the cooker. Six children shared the bath water, and just two towels.'

1940s: Homes in the War

During the **Second World War**, German planes dropped bombs all over Britain, in attacks called air raids. Thousands of people were killed and many houses were destroyed.

People at home helped with the war too. To stop any lights showing they put up blackout curtains in their windows. This meant that the enemy could not see where to bomb.

Building air raid shelters in the back garden. Everyone was given a gas mask in case of gas attacks. The toy dog at the top is wearing someone's gas mask!

> *The air raids did not break people's spirits.*
> *One air raid victim said:*
> 'Though our houses are down, our spirits are up.'

'Prefabs' were new homes built quickly from pieces made in factories for people whose homes had been bombed.

The war brought many shortages. **Rationing** was introduced to make sure that everyone got a fair share of food, clothing and furniture.

1950s: Homes for everyone

After the war, the **government** began another huge building programme. A million homes were built in five years. Each one had three bedrooms, and an indoor bathroom with a toilet.

Rationing continued for several years, but eventually new furniture and electrical goods went on sale again. The 1950s brought modern, jazzy new designs in furniture and decorations.

Many people bought their first television to watch the coronation of Queen Elizabeth in 1953.

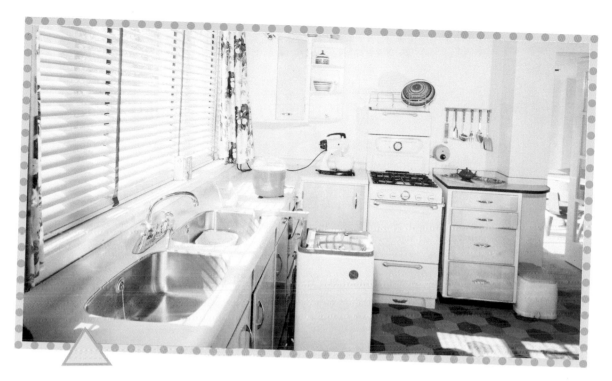

A new kitchen in the 1950s. This seemed very modern and stylish.

At this time, women were expected to leave jobs for the men and stay home to look after their families.

New household and kitchen machines were becoming more affordable. Fridges kept food fresher, and there were new **convenience foods** such as cake mixes. Can you name some convenience foods which you like to eat?

1960s: Villages in the sky

In the 1960s, modern blocks of flats, 20 or more **storeys** high were built. Street after street of unhealthy houses were knocked down to make way for new 'villages in the sky'. Would you like to live high in the sky?

This tower block was built in 1963.

Remembering skyscrapers:
'I had a love of all skyscrapers, the taller the better. I never thought what it would be like to live in one.'

At first, people were thrilled with these modern homes. But often, they missed their old **communities**, and there was nowhere safe for their children to play.

Home improvement

In the late 1960s, local **councils** started to improve houses instead. They built indoor bathrooms and new roofs. Then people could stay in their homes – and communities could stay together.

These tower blocks had lots of flats inside for people to live in.

1960s: Unfair treatment

Not everyone shared the new wealth of the 1960s. In 1966, a shocking television play called *Cathy Come Home* showed how a young woman became **homeless** and lost her children, simply because she was poor.

A scene from Cathy Come Home. *The play shocked people into setting up a charity called Shelter to demand decent housing for everyone.*

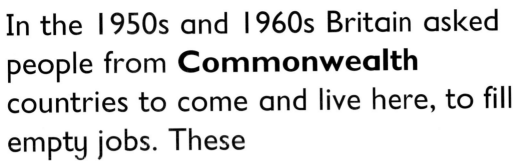

In the 1950s and 1960s Britain asked people from **Commonwealth** countries to come and live here, to fill empty jobs. These people were called immigrants. Many were forced to live in very poor homes.

A new immigrant looking for a home in the 1960s. Some immigrants faced bad treatment from landlords.

A man arriving from Jamaica in 1960 said: 'In those days housing was terrible... Sometimes two and three people lived in one room.'

1970s: DIY style

People had more money to spend in the 1970s. 'Do-it-yourself', or DIY, became a popular weekend hobby. Decoration styles used bright colours and large, bold patterns.

Bold patterns were the fashion in the 1970s.

Do you live in a town or the countryside? What do you like and dislike about it? In the 1970s, many people wanted to move out of the big cities.

Some people bought a plot of land in Wales or Scotland. Others moved to popular 'new towns', which were planned to provide good quality houses, with plenty of space.

New towns were built so that people no longer had to live in the city.

1980s: Rich and poor again

In the 1980s the **government** stopped local **councils** from building new homes to **rent**. At a time when millions of people were losing their jobs, **homelessness** became a big problem.

A family might have to wait a long time for a council home. In cities, jobless people slept on the streets because they could not afford a place to live.

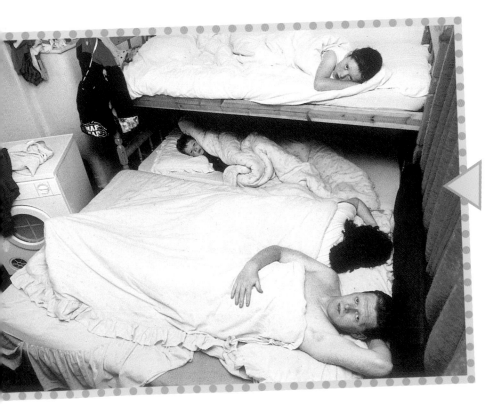

A homeless family living in one room in a cheap hotel while they wait for a council house.

Many council estates, including the tower blocks built in the 1960s, were getting run-down and very unpopular. Some were waiting to be knocked down.

In the 1980s, the gap between rich and poor seemed to be growing. Many poor people lived in bad housing while rich people were buying big new homes.

This big house was built at a time when some people had to sleep on the streets.

1990s: City or countryside?

For many years, people had been moving out of the city centres. Builders were keen to build new houses in the countryside. In the 1990s people started to say that too many fields around the edge of towns were being covered with buildings and car parks.

Old factories and warehouses were now turned into smart city flats, bringing new life back into the heart of the city.

In the 1990s, people could live in the countryside, working at home linked to their office in a town or city by telephone, fax and computer.

1900   1910

New Age travellers. There are not enough proper sites for travellers to stay on.

In the 1990s, small groups of people called New Age travellers wanted to live in a freer way, closer to nature. They moved around the country living in caravans. But local people often did not want them there.

Homes in the 21st century

What will homes be like in the 21st century? Eco-homes have been built which use clean forms of energy which will never run out, such as solar power or wind power.

All homes should be protected, so that heat and energy cannot escape through the roof or the doors and windows.

This eco-home has a big area of solar panels to catch energy from the sun.

These new style homes have been built to be less harmful to the environment. They use less energy than other houses.

The 20th century saw great improvements in British homes. But many people are still living in unhealthy conditions. **Homelessness** is still a big problem in towns and cities.

We need to find new ways to create lots of high-quality homes in lively, crowded city areas, where many people want to live and work.

Find out for yourself

Ask older people you know in your neighbourhood what they remember about growing up. Use a tape recorder or notepad to record their answers.

Your local library will have lots of books about homes in your area. Ask the librarian for help.

Find out if there is a local history society, or a branch of the housing charity, Shelter, in your area. You could write to invite a member to come and give a talk at your school.

Books

History from Photographs: Houses and Homes, Hodder Wayland, 1999
Linkers: Homes discovered through history, A & C Black, 2001

Glossary

Commonwealth the group of countries which used to be governed by Britain, including India, Pakistan, Jamaica, Australia and Canada

community a group of people who live near each other

convenience foods foods which you buy ready-prepared, or which can be cooked very quickly, to save time

council a group of people who plan and run services in their local area. A council house or flat is a home that is rented from the local council.

decade ten years. The decade of the 1910s means the ten years between 1910 and 1920.

First World War when some countries, including Britain, were at war with Germany, 1914-1918

government politicians chosen to run the country

homelessness when someone has no home to live in

pump a pipe which brings water, usually outdoors in the yard or street, for houses without taps

rationing sharing out fixed amounts of food, clothes and other goods to each person

rent money paid to live in a house or flat

Second World War when some countries, including Britain, were at war with Germany, 1939-1945

skyscrapers a tall building with many different homes inside it

storey floor of a building above the ground floor

terraced a row of houses all joined together

Index

Titles in the *What was it like in the past...?* series include:

Hardback   0 431 14826 0

Hardback   0 431 14828 7

Hardback   0 431 14827 9

Hardback   0 431 14821 X

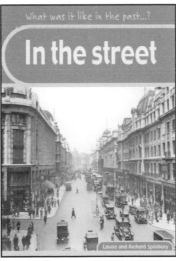

Hardback   0 431 14823 6

Hardback   0 431 14825 2

Hardback   0 431 14822 8

Hardback   0 431 14820 1

Find out about the other titles in this series on our website www.heinemann.co.uk/library